PERSEUS

RETOLD AND ILLUSTRATED BY
WARWICK HUTTON

Margaret K. McElderry Books
New York

Maxwell Macmillan Canada
Toronto

Maxwell Macmillan International
New York · Oxford · Singapore · Sydney

— for Maurice —

Margaret K. McElderry Books
Macmillan Publishing Company
866 Third Avenue
New York, NY 10022

Maxwell Macmillan Canada, Inc.
1200 Eglinton Avenue East
Suite 200
Don Mills, Ontario M3C 3N1

Macmillan Publishing Company is part of the Maxwell Communication
Group of Companies.
First edition
Printed in Singapore
10 9 8 7 6 5 4 3 2 1
The text of this book is set in Palatino.
The illustrations are rendered in watercolor and pen on paper.

Library of Congress Cataloging-in-Publication Data
Hutton, Warwick.
Perseus / retold and illustrated by Warwick
Hutton. — 1st ed.
p.   cm.
Summary: Retells the Greek myth in which the hero Perseus beheads
Medusa, the most horrible of the Gorgons.
ISBN 0-689-50565-5
1. Perseus (Greek mythology)—Juvenile literature.   2. Gorgons
(Greek mythology)—Juvenile literature.   3. Medusa (Greek
mythology)—Juvenile literature.   [1. Perseus (Greek mythology)
2. Medusa (Greek mythology) 3. Mythology, Greek.]   I. Title.
BL820.P5H85 1993   92-7639
398.21—dc20

The early morning sun rose up over the Greek island of Seriphos. It warmed Dictys's face as he looked out from his fisherman's hut on the shore. When the soft sea mist lifted, his gaze was caught by something new down at the tide line. It was a large wooden chest that must have washed up during the night. What treasure could be inside it, what riches would it hold?

The lid was not locked and it opened easily. There, to his utmost astonishment, lay the most beautiful young woman he had ever seen, holding a tiny baby. He carefully wrapped the baby in his jacket and helped the woman out.

"My name is Danaë," she said, "and this is Perseus, my son. My father put us both in this chest and pushed us out to sea. A prophecy foretold that he would be killed by his grandson, and so he set us afloat, hoping we would drown. For days and days we have been rocking and crashing in the waves." She wept as she told her story. Dictys, who was a kind and gentle man, took them both back to his home to feed and care for them.

Dictys's brother was Polydectes, king of the island, a cruel and selfish man who was used to getting his own way. Soon he began to notice Danaë's beauty and wanted her for himself. But Danaë would have nothing to do with him.

The years passed and Perseus grew up strong and tall, and as beautiful as his mother. The cruel king still wanted to have Danaë, but Perseus was in the way. He must get rid of him.

So the king planned a great celebration to which everyone was invited. Perseus knew the king's friends were as unpleasant as the king, but he went to the celebration anyhow.

Everyone brought presents for King Polydectes. When Perseus arrived, they all fell silent. "What have *you* got for me?" asked the king. Perseus flushed red, for he had nothing to give. All the courtiers began to laugh. In desperation, he said, "I will bring you anything you want—if you will leave my mother alone." The king looked around at his friends. For a moment, he seemed to ponder. Then, smiling cruelly, he said, "You must fetch me Medusa's head."

Perseus knew he had been tricked and humiliated. He left and ran down to the seashore, his face burning with anger. What or who was Medusa?

As he looked out at the waves, the gods Athene and Hermes appeared from the evening mist. Perseus had never before seen any gods. To his surprise Athene spoke, in a strong gentle voice. "We will help you to get Medusa's head," she said. Perseus listened in astonishment. "First you must go to the Gray Sisters. Somehow you must make them tell you where the Stygian Nymphs are. They, in turn, will say where the Gorgons' valley is. When you get there you will find three Gorgons. The most horrible of all is Medusa. Her face is so terrible that just a glimpse of it turns people to stone. To survive, you must borrow my polished shield and only look at her reflection in it."

"Use this too," Hermes added, and he held out a weapon that glinted in the evening light. "It is my adamantine sickle, so sharp and hard it will cut through anything on earth."

Perseus set off the next morning in great excitement. Following the gods' directions, he soon found the cave where the Gray Sisters lived. They were revolting—old, wrinkled, and with long filthy gray hair. They sat together, arguing and complaining as they passed something back and forth.

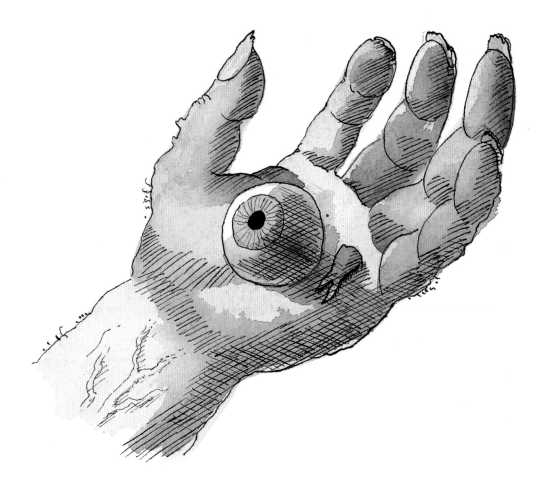

Perseus crept closer and saw, in one clawlike hand, a single eyeball and an old brown tooth. It was the only eye and the only tooth the Sisters had between them, and they took turns using them. Perseus waited patiently, and then, in the middle of an argument they were having, he darted forward and snatched up the eyeball and tooth.

Now all three of the Sisters were blind and toothless.
They thrashed their hands in the air and screeched at each
other.

"Tell me where the Stygian Nymphs live and I will
return your eye and your tooth to you," Perseus said.

He was soon on his way again. This journey was much
longer, and Perseus was tired when he reached the
Nymphs. They were very beautiful, and their land was
like paradise. As they gently cared for him, they told him
the way to the Gorgons' valley.

He had a long night's rest to gather his strength, and in the morning, before the Nymphs sent him on his way, they gave him a bag, a cap, and a pair of winged sandals. "The bag is to put Medusa's head in when you cut it off. The cap will make you invisible, and the sandals will let you fly from the fury of the other two Gorgons."

As he traveled on, Perseus thought of his mother and Dictys the fisherman, and wondered what the cruel king was doing to them. The land around him grew drier, hotter and more stony. The larger stones looked curiously like people and animals. This was the Valley of the Gorgons. The sun shone down strongly. Perseus walked more cautiously, and there, at last, in an untidy pile on the ground, he saw the monsters, fast asleep. But the snakes in their hair were awake, and they hissed venomously as he crept up. Carefully, looking only in Athene's bright shield, Perseus picked out the horrifying face of Medusa. The snakes darted at his ankles as, with one mighty stroke of the sickle, he hacked off her head.

He kept his eyes closed while he put the head in the bag given him by the Nymphs, and then in horror watched as the other Gorgons awoke. He jammed the cap on his head, thrust his feet into the winged sandals, and jumped into the air.

The most terrible screams and howls trailed away below him as he flew up and ever upward, until like a great invisible swallow, he curved south, away from that awful valley.

High above Africa Perseus flew. He could see the Atlas Mountains below, and then the Sahara Desert. He came lower over Ethiopia, and, as he skimmed on toward the sea, he noticed a figure on the rocky coast below. Down, down he flew, until he could see, to his astonishment, that a beautiful girl was chained to the rocks, unclothed and undefended. She was weeping in distress. As he landed, he took off his cap. The girl's eyes opened wide when, from nowhere—out of the air—Perseus appeared beside her.

Perseus spoke to her gently. "Why are you chained here?"

"My name is Andromeda. My mother boasted that she and I were more beautiful than the Sea Nymphs. In their anger, the Nymphs sent a sea monster to ravage the coast. At last, to protect his people, my father, who is the king, has chained me here as a sacrifice."

At that very moment, the monster rose from the sea. Its vast head dripped with seaweed, and its great jaws opened wide. Quickly, Perseus reached inside the bag. Closing his eyes and covering Andromeda's, he held out Medusa's head to face the sea monster. There was a groan and a creak. In seconds the monster had turned into stone. Then slowly it sank until only a ridge of rocks marked where it had been.

With the sickle, Perseus cut Andromeda's chains. He put his arms tightly around her and, with his winged sandals, lifted her up to the clifftop, where her parents had been watching. When Perseus asked for Andromeda as his bride, they agreed at once.

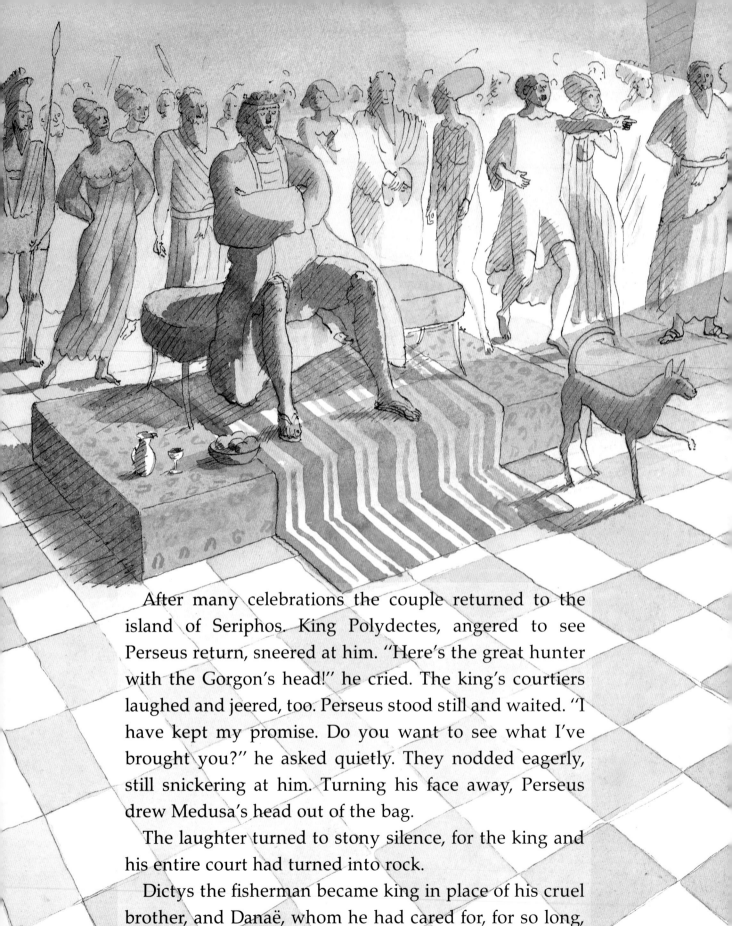

After many celebrations the couple returned to the island of Seriphos. King Polydectes, angered to see Perseus return, sneered at him. "Here's the great hunter with the Gorgon's head!" he cried. The king's courtiers laughed and jeered, too. Perseus stood still and waited. "I have kept my promise. Do you want to see what I've brought you?" he asked quietly. They nodded eagerly, still snickering at him. Turning his face away, Perseus drew Medusa's head out of the bag.

The laughter turned to stony silence, for the king and his entire court had turned into rock.

Dictys the fisherman became king in place of his cruel brother, and Danaë, whom he had cared for, for so long, agreed to become his queen.

That evening Perseus and Andromeda sat dreaming by the shore. He told her of his childhood, and how he had arrived in Seriphos in the wooden chest. As they gazed out to sea, the evening mist rolled in, and suddenly Athene and Hermes appeared again. Perseus stood up and thanked them for all their help. He gave everything back to them: the cap, the sandals, the shield and sickle—and the bag with Medusa's head in it. The gods vanished into the night and Perseus put his arm once more around Andromeda.

What happened to the head of Medusa? It was set into
Athene's shield to strike terror into her enemies.